Keeping Unusual Pets

Ferrets

June McNicholas

Heinemann
LIBRARY

Chicago, Illinois

www.heinemannraintree.com
Visit our website to find out more information about Heinemann-Raintree books.

To order:
☎ Phone 888-454-2279
🖥 Visit www.heinemannraintree.com to browse our catalog and order online.

© 2002, 2010 Heinemann Library
an imprint of Capstone Global Library, LLC
Chicago, Illinois

Edited by Louise Galpine and Laura Knowles
Designed by Kim Miracle and Victoria Bevan
Picture research by Mica Brancic
Originated by Capstone Global Library Ltd 2010
Printed and bound in China by Leo Paper Products Ltd

14 13 12 11 10
10 9 8 7 6 5 4 3 2 1

Library of Congress Cataloging-in-Publication Data
McNicholas, June, 1956-
  Ferrets / June McNicholas. -- 2nd ed.
    p. cm. -- (Keeping unusual pets)
  Includes bibliographical references and index.
  ISBN 978-1-4329-3848-2 (hc)
  1. Ferrets as pets--Juvenile literature. I. Title.
  SF459.F47M36 2010
  636.976'628--dc22
                    2009035276

Acknowledgments
The author and publisher are grateful to the following for permission to reproduce copyright material: © Capstone Global Library Ltd pp. **5, 8, 11, 13, 15 top, 15 bottom, 16 left, 17 top, 19 top, 20 top, 20 bottom, 21 top, 21 bottom, 22 top, 22 bottom, 23 bottom, 24 bottom, 25 top, 26, 27, 28, 29 top, 29 bottom, 30 top, 31 top, 32, 33 top, 33 bottom, 34, 35, 36, 37, 39, 40, 41, 42, 43 top, 44 left, 44 right, 45 top, 45 bottom** (Aylesbury Studios/Dave Bradford); © Capstone Publishers pp. **4 top, 9, 10, 12 top, 14 top, 16 right, 18, 19 bottom, 24 top, 25 bottom, 31 bottom,** (Karon Dubke); Corbis pp. **4 bottom** (© George McCarthy), **7** (© Jeff Vanuga); Istockphoto p. **38** (© Brad Wynnyk); Manor Farm Woodcraft p. **17 bottom**; Shutterstock p. **43 bottom** (© Couperfield); © The Bridgeman Art Library p. **6** (British Library).

Cover photograph of a 10-week-old ferret kit reproduced with permission of Shutterstock (© Eric Isselée).

We would like to thank Judy Tuma and Rob Lee for their invaluable help in the preparation of this book.

Every effort has been made to contact copyright holders of material reproduced in this book. Any omissions will be rectified in subsequent printings if notice is given to the publisher.

Disclaimer
All the Internet addresses (URLs) given in this book were valid at the time of going to press. However, due to the dynamic nature of the Internet, some addresses may have changed, or sites may have changed or ceased to exist since publication. While the author and publisher regret any inconvenience this may cause readers, no responsibility for any such changes can be accepted by either the author or the publisher.

No animals were harmed during the process of taking photographs for this series.

Contents

What Is a Ferret? 4

Ferret Facts 6

Is a Ferret for You? 8

Choosing Your Ferret 10

What Do I Need? 12

Caring for Your Ferret 18

Becoming Friends 24

Fun and Games 28

Staying Healthy 34

Some Health Problems 36

Saying Goodbye 42

Keeping a Record 44

Glossary 46

Find Out More 47

Index 48

Any words appearing in the text in bold, **like this**, are explained in the glossary.

What is a Ferret?

The pet ferrets we have today are descendants of animals **domesticated** thousands of years ago. The rare, wild black-footed ferret that lives in the United States is a distant relative of our pet ferrets. Pet ferrets do not behave like wild animals and are not usually afraid of people.

Ferrets are **mammals**, which means they are **warm-blooded** (they produce their own body heat). They give birth to live babies and feed their babies with milk. Ferrets belong to the **mustelid** family, which includes stoats, weasels, polecats, otters, pine martens, wolverines, skunks, and badgers.

Domesticated ferrets can be friendly and fun pets.

Strong smells

Ferrets have small scent glands all over their body, and fully grown ferrets can have a strong smell. Mustelids also have special scent glands under their tail. These glands can give off a really bad smell if the ferret is very frightened, defending itself, or hurt. The smell passes quickly and helps the ferret protect itself, so it is a good thing!

Polecats are wild animals that are closely related to ferrets.

Working ferrets

Ferrets are excellent hunters and love chasing through tunnels. Drawings survive from the 11th century showing women using ferrets to help them chase rabbits out of their burrows and into waiting nets. Today, in some parts of the world, ferrets are still used to hunt rabbits.

Ferrets are used as working animals in many parts of the world, but they also make playful and intelligent pets.

NEED TO KNOW

✪ Ferrets are not wild animals, so you do not need a license to own them.

✪ Children are not allowed to buy pets themselves. You should always have an adult with you when you buy your pet.

✪ Most countries have laws protecting animals. It is your responsibility to make sure your ferret is healthy and well cared for. Always take your pet to the vet if it is sick or injured.

✪ You are legally responsible for your ferret's care and its behavior. Think about **insuring** your ferret. You can find out about insurance for your pet through ferret groups (see page 47).

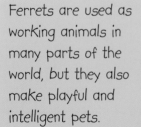

Ferret Facts

Ferrets are very playful and enjoy human company. They can be **housebroken** so they will not make a mess on your floor. They make very little noise and they do not chew wires or cables. Ferrets are not **nocturnal**, so they tend to be awake at the same time you are.

This painting from the 1300s shows people using a ferret to catch a rabbit.

FERRET HISTORY

No one knows for sure where the ancestors of the domestic ferret came from. We do know, however, that as far back as 2,000 years ago ferrets were used as hunters. The ferrets' long, low bodies allowed them to enter burrows to flush out rabbits. In the 1400s, ferrets became popular pets in important European homes and castles. Approximately 300 years ago, ferrets were brought to North America. At that time some were still used for hunting. Today, ferrets are popular pets in Europe and the United States.

Ferrets are usually born in the spring and early summer. Young ferrets are called **kits**. The average life span of a ferret is about seven years, although many live for up to ten years and some live even longer.

Hobs and jills

Male ferrets are called **hobs** and female ferrets are called **jills**. Hobs are usually larger than jills. They weigh around 1.5 to 2.2 kilograms (53 to 78 ounces) and are about 45 to 60 centimeters (18 to 24 inches) long. Jills weigh around 500 grams to 1.5 kilograms (18 to 53 ounces) and are about 30 to 40 centimeters (12 to 16 inches) long. Both hobs and jills gain a lot of extra weight in the winter. They sometimes gain more than a quarter of their total summer body weight, but they soon lose it again.

Ferrets under threat

The wild black-footed ferret is a close relative of the domestic ferret, but it is in danger of becoming **extinct** in its native habitat. Why has this happened? First, the numbers of prairie dogs, their main food source, have fallen dramatically. Another reason is that black-footed ferrets are prey for large birds such as golden eagles and great-horned owls. Coyotes are predators, too. Black-footed ferrets can catch **canine distemper**, a disease that kills them. In order to save this species, black-footed ferrets are being raised in captivity and then released into the wild. With careful conservation efforts, maybe the black-footed ferret will survive in the wild.

The black-footed ferret is now extremely rare and is in danger of becoming extinct.

Is a Ferret for You?

Ferrets can look cute and fun, but are they the right pet for you? Are you the right person to be a ferret owner? If you and your ferret do not suit one another, you may make one another very unhappy. You need to think carefully before you decide to get a ferret.

As with any pet, there are good things and not-so-good things about owning a ferret. Here are some of the things that you should think about.

GOOD POINTS

- ✪ Ferrets are intelligent.
- ✪ Ferrets are playful and entertaining.
- ✪ Ferrets can live for seven years or more.
- ✪ Ferrets can live indoors or outdoors.
- ✪ Ferrets are not **nocturnal**, so they are active when you are.
- ✪ Ferrets are naturally clean: they usually only use one corner of their housing as a toilet.
- ✪ Ferrets will play in the house with you.
- ✪ Ferrets can be taken for walks on a **harness**.

Many people enjoy having **inquisitive** ferrets as pets.

Ferrets are not naturally destructive, but they are playful and inquisitive. If they can reach something, they may wreck it!

NOT-SO-GOOD POINTS

✪ Ferrets have a noticeable smell. This is not usually a problem in **neutered** animals, but some people find it unpleasant.

✪ Even neutered ferrets can give off a very bad smell if they are frightened or hurt.

✪ It can be expensive to set up your ferret's home.

✪ You will have to exercise and play with your ferret for at least two hours a day.

✪ Ferrets need to have their cage cleaned out and be given food and water at least once a day.

✪ A ferret can bite hard if it is frightened or hurt.

✪ Your ferret will need regular **vaccinations** and health checkups and may need to be treated for illnesses. Visits to the vet can be expensive.

Yes or no?

Can you handle all these jobs? Now is the time to be honest with yourself. If the answer is "no," then maybe you should think of an easier pet to own.

Can you make a promise to your future ferret to be responsible for its health and happiness? Will you care for it even when you are in a hurry or want to do something else? If the answer is "yes," you may have just made the decision to own a ferret.

Choosing Your Ferret

It is important to meet and handle as many ferrets as you can before you finally decide to be a ferret owner. You could try contacting ferret clubs (see page 47) to find out where and when events are being held. If you attend those events, you will have the opportunity to talk to ferret owners and meet their pets.

One ferret or two?

Ferrets like to have company, so it is usually best to have two **neutered** ferrets (ferrets that have had an operation to stop them from **breeding**). Try to buy them together as youngsters. It is possible to introduce adult ferrets to each other, but this should be done gradually. You may need the advice of an experienced ferret owner to make sure your ferrets become friends with one another. If you can only have one ferret, you will have to make sure that you give it all the time and company it needs.

Hob or jill?

Both **hobs** and **jills** make good pets, but both sexes should be neutered. At the same time they should be **de-scented**. This will allow you to keep hobs and jills together. If your ferret is not already neutered when you buy it, you will need to take it to the vet for a simple operation (see page 35). Neutered ferrets can live happily in same-sex or mixed-sex groups.

Take your time choosing your ferret. You and your pet will have to like each other and live together for many years!

Buying your ferret

You should buy your ferret from someone who has been recommended to you by another ferret owner, by a member of a ferret club, or by your vet. It is not a good idea to buy from pet stores unless they can tell you where the ferret came from. The store owner should also be able to show you how well the ferret can be handled. Never buy ferrets from other places, such as an ad in the newspaper, as they may not have been cared for properly.

WHAT TO LOOK FOR

It is best to buy a young ferret, but **kits** should be at least eight weeks old, and preferably ten weeks, before they leave their mother. Whether you are looking for a kit or an adult, there are a few basic things to look out for. The ferret should:

- ✪ be living in clean surroundings
- ✪ have bright eyes, clean ears, and a soft, clean coat
- ✪ be friendly and not frightened of you
- ✪ be willing to be handled.

TOP TIP

Watch how the person who is looking after the ferrets picks them up. If the ferret-keeper is experienced, the ferrets will probably be used to being handled.

This ferret has bright eyes and looks lively and alert. If it can be easily handled, it would make a good pet.

What Do I Need?

The two most important pieces of equipment you will need for your ferret are a strong cage or hutch and a secure play area.

The cage

Your ferret's cage will be its main home. Ferrets are active, so you must have a roomy cage. For one or two ferrets, the cage should be at least 120 centimeters (48 inches) wide, 90 cm (36 in.) deep, and 60 cm (24 in.) high, or even bigger. Ferrets are strong animals, so most rabbit hutches, for example, will need to be fitted with extra-strong wire and door catches to make them ferret-proof. The cage will also need a separate sleeping area for when the ferrets need privacy and quiet.

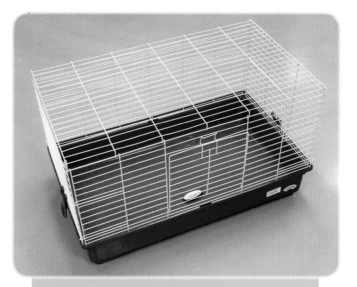

Many pet stores sell metal cages such as the one above, or wooden hutches such as the one below. Either type can make a good home for a ferret.

Indoors or out?

Ferrets can live indoors or outside in a shed. If your ferret is going to live indoors, put its cage somewhere where it will not be in cold drafts. Ferrets do not like being too hot, so do not put the cage close to a radiator. It is also important to make sure that the cage is not in a place where other animals can bother or frighten your ferret.

Some people choose to keep ferrets outdoors in a shed or sheltered area. The cage must be protected from wind, rain, and other bad weather. A weatherproof cover is essential to put over the hutch. Ferrets should not be exposed to temperatures over 27°Celsius (80°Fahrenheit). Ferrets can die from **heatstroke**, so make sure that your ferret has plenty of shade in hot weather. Remember that an outdoor ferret also needs to be safe from wild animals such as foxes, as well as from neighboring cats and dogs.

TOP TIPS

- ✪ Wooden cages are best, with a solid wood floor.

- ✪ Avoid cages with wire-mesh floors, because they are uncomfortable for a ferret's soft feet.

- ✪ A two-story cage will give lots of space and height for an upstairs bedroom, a ramp, and downstairs feeding, play, and bathroom areas.

Cage furnishings

Before you bring your ferret home, make sure you have everything it will need to settle into its new cage.

A cozy bed

The sleeping area should have a box to act as a bed with blankets to burrow into. Do not use material with loose fibers that can catch on your ferret's claws. Do not use straw or hay for your ferret's bedding. These materials can contain **ticks** and other **external parasites**.

FERRET TOYS

Your ferret will enjoy having some toys. Try some of these:

- ✪ tubes that are wide enough to run through
- ✪ shredded paper, small towels, or paper bags
- ✪ a hammock to bounce in or sleep in
- ✪ a ball on a rope (hung from the cage ceiling)
- ✪ a cat ball with a bell in it.

You can use a wooden crate and some old T-shirts and towels to make a cozy bed for your ferret.

Food and water bowls

You will need two bowls—one for food and another for water. The bowls should be heavy enough that your ferret cannot turn them upside down, or the type that clip onto the wires of the cage. Most ferrets think their water bowl is for paddling in and love splashing the water around! If you don't mind the puddles, let your ferrets enjoy playing with water, but make sure they always have enough to drink by clipping a water bottle to the wire of their cage.

Litter corner

Ferrets usually use only one corner of their cage as a toilet. This is most often the corner farthest away from their bed. Your ferret will decide which corner it wants—and you won't be able to change its mind. Put a litter tray filled with dust-free clumping cat litter or newspaper in this corner. Remember to clean it out at least once a day.

Ferrets love to play with bowls and tubs, so make sure that your pet's food bowl is too heavy for it to overturn.

Some ferrets learn to use cat litter trays, but others just kick the tray out of the way. If this happens, you could try using cat litter in the litter corner, but most ferrets will have fun throwing it around.

Your ferret will have hours of fun bouncing around in a hammock. You can make a hammock from an old sleeping bag or pillowcase.

Exercise areas

Your ferret will need regular playtimes of two to three hours each day out of its cage, either in the house with you or in an outdoor run. The advantage of letting your ferret play indoors is that it will become part of the family and everyone can enjoy it. The disadvantage is that you will need to "ferret-proof" your home.

A ferret-proof home

If you let your ferret run around inside, make sure it cannot climb into fireplaces, get trapped behind furniture, or get stuck inside cabinets. Always let other members of the family know that your ferret is out of its cage. You do not want them stepping on your pet or leaving doors open for it to escape.

Never leave your ferret alone, because you can never tell what it will get into. Move houseplants and anything breakable out of the way. Some ferrets scratch at carpets, especially in front of doors. A rug, sheet of newspaper, or piece of heavy, plastic carpet protector can stop any damage.

Some strong **hobs** learn how to open cabinets and refrigerators.

An open drawer or cabinet can be an invitation to play!

Ferrets are not interested in plants and flowers. They just want to scatter the soil as far as possible!

An outdoor run

A run with an area measuring 1 meter by 2 meters (3 feet by 6½ feet) will be large enough for a couple of ferrets. Strong mesh on a timber frame will make a good framework for a run. The floor will need to be mesh, too, to stop ferrets from digging tunnels or squeezing underneath the frame. A solid covering should be placed over the mesh to stop the ferret's tiny paws and nails from getting caught in the mesh. Ferrets can climb well, so fix a strong top or lid onto the run that can be bolted down.

Put a bedding box inside the run and lots of toys and things to climb on. Do not forget to provide food and water. Put the run in a sheltered area, protected from cold winds, heavy rain, and hot sun. You can use a strong **tarpaulin**, or tarp, to give extra cover.

Ferrets will enjoy being outdoors in mild weather, but your pet will still need human company, and you must make time every day to handle your ferret and play with it.

Caring for Your Ferret

Ferrets are **carnivorous** animals, which means they eat meat. But meat is not enough on its own. The best food to give your pet is a specially made dried food for ferrets. This contains all the **protein** and **vitamins** your ferret needs to stay healthy, and it is more **hygienic** than raw meat. Your ferret's food should contain one-third animal protein and one-fifth fat. Do not feed your ferret cat or dog food. The pieces are larger than ferret food pieces and could get stuck in your pet's throat. They may also not contain enough protein for ferrets. Never feed your ferret bread and milk. Many ferrets get an upset stomach if they drink milk.

TOP TIPS

- ✪ There are several good ferret foods that you can buy. Whichever one you choose, always follow the instructions on the package.

- ✪ Unless your ferret is very greedy, you can leave a bowl of dried food in its cage all the time so it can help itself.

- ✪ Many ferrets like to eat small amounts, rather than a large meal all at once.

Your ferret will love munching on its dried food.

Not too much

Do not overfeed your ferret—you do not want a fat, lazy ferret! Most ferrets are good at eating the right amount and do not become overweight, but some can be greedy, so you need to be aware of their eating habits. Remember that most ferrets will gain a lot of weight in the winter, but if your pet gets very fat, it may be eating too much. If your ferret has a fat stomach but it is not eating a lot, take it to see a vet. Sometimes this can be a sign of illness.

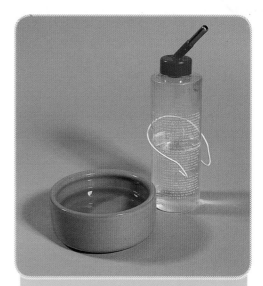

Make sure your ferret has fresh water every day. You can use a heavy bowl or a large bottle that clips onto the outside of the cage.

A small piece of fruit can be a very special treat.

Treats

Some ferrets love treats, but you need to be careful not to feed them things that are bad for them. It is best to buy tasty treats and **vitamin supplements** that are specially made for ferrets. Candy and chocolates are particularly bad for ferrets. They can make a ferret very fat and give it tooth problems. Suitable healthy treats are a little boiled egg or a little piece of banana or apple.

Keeping clean

Your ferret's litter corner should be cleaned at least daily. Once a week you should clean and wipe all the surfaces in your ferret's cage with a cloth soaked in a mild disinfectant. Once a day the food bowl and water bottle should be washed and your pet's bedding checked to make sure it is clean and dry. Bedding and hammocks should be changed and washed every week.

Grooming

Ferrets **groom** their own fur, but twice a year they lose a large amount of their old coat and grow new fur. This is called **molting**.

Hold your ferret firmly while you shampoo its fur.

After you have finished shampooing your ferret, rinse it thoroughly and then dry it.

BATH TIME

Ferrets rarely need bathing. If your ferret gets dirty, or if you are taking it to a show, you can wash it with a special ferret shampoo.

- ✪ Do not cover the ferret in water— just dip it in lukewarm water and then hold it above the water.

- ✪ Gently shampoo your ferret's coat, avoiding its face and eyes.

- ✪ Dip it back in the water to rinse it.

- ✪ Dry it with a clean towel and then stand back while it runs around the room to get really dry!

- ✪ Do not let your ferret get cold, and make sure it is absolutely dry before going outside.

Nail care

Ferrets' nails grow quite quickly, so you will need to cut them regularly. Place your ferret's paw flat on the palm of your hand. If its nails dig into your hand they need cutting. Having its nails cut does not hurt the ferret, but most ferrets do not like it much. It is a good idea to get another person to hold the ferret while you do the trimming.

Most ferrets have pale nails, so it is easy to see the red vein in each claw. Do not clip too close to this vein, as it will pinch and hurt the ferret or even make it bleed. Use ordinary nail clippers and cut just a little way below the vein.

This ferret's nails are the correct length.

It can help to give your ferret a treat while its nails are being trimmed. There are lots of tasty liquid vitamin treats that will keep your pet occupied.

TOP TIP

It can be easier to use a dry shampoo, made especially for animals, on your ferret than to wash it in water. Dry shampoo is a powder that is brushed into the ferret's coat and then brushed out again. Dry shampooing is a good idea when the weather is very cold, or for ferrets that hate baths.

CHECKING YOUR FERRET

It is important that you check your ferret regularly to make sure it is fit and well.

- ✪ Check your ferret all over each day for any lumps, bumps, or sore spots.

- ✪ Check that your ferret's teeth are clean and its gums are a healthy pink.

- ✪ Check your pet's nails to see that they are not broken or too long.

- ✪ Check your ferret's litter corner for any unusual **feces.**

- ✪ Check for fleas and **ticks**, especially if your ferret goes out for walks in fields or is in contact with cats, dogs, or other animals.

- ✪ Check that your pet's ears are clean. A weekly wipe with a tissue is usually all that is needed. Never prod inside a ferret's ears with cotton swabs.

- ✪ If you find anything unusual, the information on pages 36 to 41 may help you.

These are normal ferret feces. If your ferret's feces look abnormal, you should tell an adult and contact a vet.

You can buy special ear-cleaning tissues from pet stores to wipe inside your pet's ears. Do it very gently and never poke anything inside an animal's ears.

Vacation care

Ferrets need daily care. If you are away for a short period, such as a couple of days, it is probably best to ask a friend or neighbor to visit your ferret every day to clean out its cage and give it food, water, and exercise. Choose someone who knows and likes your ferret and whom you can trust to look after your pet for you. Make sure you show the person how to care for your pet and leave clear written instructions about exercise times, how much food to give, and when to feed your pet. Write down your phone number and the vet's phone number in case there is an emergency.

For longer periods you will need to find someone who will **board** your ferret. Ferret clubs often have details of people willing to board ferrets. Make your arrangements well in advance, especially as some places insist that your ferret has up-to-date **vaccinations**.

Going on vacation

Some people take their ferret on vacation with them. Your ferret will need a secure pet carrier and a suitable cage to live in while it is on vacation. If you take your pet for a walk, be sure it has your vacation address and telephone number on its collar or **harness**, in case it gets lost.

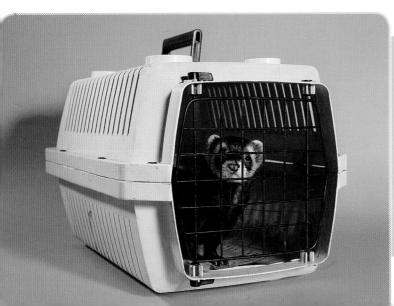

You can take your ferret on very short trips in a pet carrier like this one. Remember to put some food, a water bottle, and a blanket in its carrier if you are traveling more than a few miles.

Becoming Friends

Do not expect instant friendship with your ferret. It takes time to get to know one another. Your pet will need to settle into its cage for a day or two before you start to handle it.

Easy does it

Start by talking to your ferret while it is in its cage so that it gets used to your voice. Do not try to handle it if it is hungry or tired. Hungry ferrets mistake fingers for food, and tired ferrets may be grumpy. Gently offer your pet a healthy treat.

Do not touch your ferret while it is eating. Avoid making sudden movements or noises that might startle it.

Picking up your ferret

When you are sure your ferret is ready to be touched, pick it up with one hand behind its front legs and the other hand supporting its bottom. If it relaxes, you can support its bottom against your body and stroke it with your free hand. Do not rush things. You both need time to learn to trust one another. With time, you will be able to hold your pet over your arm or lying in your arms on its back like a baby.

Use one hand to hold your ferret behind its front legs and the other to support its bottom.

Special care

If you get an adult ferret from a shelter, it may have had unkind owners in the past, so you will have to teach it to trust people again. This requires extra time and patience, but it is very worthwhile in the end, so don't give up.

Meeting other pets

Ferrets can get along well with cats and dogs, but the first time you introduce them make sure your ferret is safely in its cage. This is a safe way to see how they will react to each other. Ferrets are natural hunters of rabbits and small animals, so you should never let them near pet rabbits, guinea pigs, hamsters, rats, gerbils, or other small animals or birds.

TOP TIP

Do not put your ferret near your face until it is completely happy about being picked up. Some ferrets grab noses and chins!

Before too long your ferret should relax and become very friendly!

Your ferret can become good friends with your cat or dog, but never leave them together without supervision.

Nip or bite?

There is a difference between a ferret nip and a bite. Ferrets use their teeth in play, and they do not always know that these play nips can hurt you. **Kits** are especially nippy because they can be over excitable—just like human children.

Do not punish a ferret of any age for nipping or biting you. Distract your pet by offering it an interesting toy such as something for it to chase or jump on. Then pick up your ferret and stroke it gently and soothingly until it calms down. A good tip is to feed your ferret before you handle it. That way it will not be hungry enough to think that your hand is food, and it will be too full to get too excitable.

Your ferret may sometimes get over excited and give you a small nip. These play nips do not usually hurt.

Painful bites

A real bite is painful. The ferret may hang on to your hand and really sink its teeth in. This usually happens because your ferret is hurt or frightened, or because it is not ready to trust people yet. Do not be too upset. Just start again by making friends slowly with your ferret. It is very rare for a ferret to remain bad tempered if it is treated kindly. If you need any help, call a ferret club (see page 47) for advice. They have lots of experience in helping new owners.

Hanging on

Occasionally, a ferret might hold your finger firmly without biting, but still show no signs of wanting to let go. It probably wants to take you somewhere. Let it lead you wherever it wants. It will let go of your finger when it gets bored, although it may try stuffing you into its play tube or dragging you under the sofa first!

Use a toy to distract your ferret if it is being nippy. Then stroke it gently until it calms down.

TOP TIP

Always be patient with your ferret. It is better to take things very slowly and get it right than to rush it. If you make a mistake, it will upset you and your ferret and will take time to get on track again.

Fun and Games

Ferrets are fun-loving creatures and need lots of playtime and toys. It will be up to you to stop your ferret from getting fat, lazy, and bored.

How ferrets play

Ferrets play by bouncing, pouncing, and rolling around on the floor. They do a lot of sideways dancing, often with their mouths open, and while they dance they make little hissing or chuckling noises. Ferrets will pretend to attack you or anything that moves. It sometimes looks as if they are chasing something that only they can see!

A friend for your ferret?

Play is very important to ferrets, so think about how to keep your pet occupied. The best thing for a ferret to play with is another ferret, so consider owning two ferrets if possible. Ferrets are sociable animals and like the company of other ferrets. Two ferrets can be twice as much fun for their owner.

When ferrets play, they can look as if they have gone completely crazy! Some people call the way they play "the weasel war-dance."

One ferret

If you can only have one ferret, you will have to make sure that you give your pet all the time and company it needs. Otherwise it could get lonely. You could think about contacting a shelter. They often have ferrets that have always lived on their own and need to be kept as a single pet.

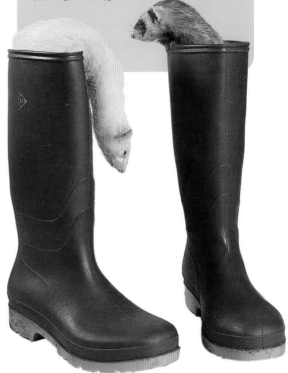

Your ferret will probably enjoy exploring an old pair of rubber boots.

PLAYTIME

Whether you have one ferret or two, you will still need to give your pet exercise and playtime.

- ✪ Make sure you have a secure area where your ferret can play safely.

- ✪ Spend some time every day having fun with your ferret.

- ✪ You could try ferret racing games with tubes and tunnels. Some ferret clubs have special races, although they are held more for fun than for serious competition.

Ferrets love racing through tubes. You could set up a complete obstacle course for your pet, with tubes to chase through and blocks to climb over.

Toys for your ferret

There are lots of ferret toys in pet stores, but you can make your own much more cheaply. This means you can give your pet a change of toys. Ferrets can get bored if they play with the same toys all the time.

Digging and burrowing

Ferrets will enjoy burrowing into a good-sized bowl of dry soil—but this is a bit messy, so check with your family first!

Ferrets love playing with crinkly paper bags.

FERRET FAVORITES

- ✪ Tubes and tunnels: These are real favorites. You can use drainpipes or tubes that have been used for carpet rolls. Make sure that they are wide enough before you give them to your ferret to play with.

- ✪ Large crinkly paper bags: Ferrets love the noise they make. NEVER let your ferret play with plastic bags.

- ✪ Hammocks: Make a hammock from an old sleeping bag, a pillowcase, or something similar. Do not use anything with loose threads that a ferret's nails can get caught in. Tie or hook each corner of the hammock to the top of the ferret cage or play area. Your ferret will use it like a trampoline!

Water play

Some ferrets love to splash in water, but others hate it. Use a wide, shallow, heavy bowl that a ferret can paddle in and out of comfortably. Some ferrets will "snorkel" by putting their noses under water and blowing bubbles. Others try to "dig'" at the water. Only allow ferrets to play in water in warm weather and always dry them thoroughly before putting them back in their cage.

Other toys

Your ferret will enjoy other toys, such as cat balls, toys hung from the cage roof, or just bundles of shredded paper. Your ferret will spend lots of time unwrapping packages, especially if there is lots of noisy paper to play with.

Try dangling a ball on a string just above your ferret. Soon it will be leaping and twisting to grab at the ball.

SAFETY FIRST

Never give your ferret toys made from soft rubber or sponge. It might take bites out of these, and pieces could get stuck in its throat or stomach. Also avoid soft, woolly materials that can catch on its claws.

Boxes with ferret-sized holes cut into them are a lot of fun for your pets.

Walking your ferret

Some ferrets love walks. Others just refuse to cooperate, although some enjoy being carried around. It is unkind to force an unwilling ferret to go for walks.

You will need a **harness** and a leash. Choose a brightly colored harness and attach a tag with your name, phone number, and address on it. If your ferret does get lost, someone might find it and be able to contact you.

TOP TIPS

- ✪ Most dogs will never have seen a ferret and may want to chase it or snap at it. Pick up your ferret long before a dog comes close.

- ✪ Do not let your ferret go down holes or in places where you cannot safely reach it.

- ✪ Do not walk your ferret on hot, sunny days or if it is very cold or wet. A short playtime in snow is a real treat, but do not let your ferret get cold.

Buy a harness with two straps. Fit one strap over the head and fasten the second strap behind the front legs. Then attach the leash securely.

Where will we go?

A ferret will expect you to go wherever it wants! Just when you think you are going in a straight line, your ferret may dive into the undergrowth or show that it wants to be picked up.

After a walk, always check your ferret for bits of twig or grass that may get matted into its coat. Check for fleas or **ticks** if you have been walking in areas where there are farm animals or wild animals.

Ferrets tend to walk better on a path or a track. Open fields seem to confuse them. This may be because they have very poor eyesight. Ferrets will often recognize a familiar path and pull ahead on their leash, almost running.

Make sure your ferret is clean, dry, and comfortable after its walk and give it a snack and a drink. Then settle it down in its cage for a well-earned rest. You will probably need the same!

Staying Healthy

Apart from you, the most important person in your ferret's life is its vet. You may already know a vet who specializes in ferrets in your area, or other ferret owners may have recommended one to you. You can also contact local ferret groups for a list of vets who have experience caring for ferrets (see page 47).

There are two very important things you need to do to keep your ferret healthy. One is getting it **vaccinated** once a year, and the other is having it **neutered** and **de-scented**. You will need to visit your vet to get these things done. Your vet will talk to you and your parents or guardians about why they are necessary.

PROTECT YOUR PET!

Your ferret will need a yearly vaccination against **canine distemper**. This is done by your vet. The injection is very important if your ferret is in contact with dogs or visits places where dogs walk. It is a simple injection that will protect your ferret from a disease that could kill it.

This jill has just been spayed. You can see where she was shaved for her operation and the tiny stitches that close the cut.

Neutering

Ferret experts do not recommend **breeding**. A **jill** may give birth to as many as 12 **kits**, and it can be difficult to find good homes for all of them. It is much better for you and your ferret if you have it neutered.

Neutering is an operation that stops ferrets from breeding. The operation is called **castration** when it is done on a **hob**, and **spaying** when done on a jill. Apart from preventing unwanted babies, neutering has other advantages. Hobs become more friendly and playful. Jills are protected from some illnesses. Ferrets cope with the operation very well and recover quickly after resting for a few days.

Some Health Problems

You have many responsibilities to properly care for your ferrets. As you care for them, here are some of the common problems you might experience.

Litter problems

Each time you clear out your ferret's litter corner, check its **feces** to see if they look normal (see picture on page 22). If the feces are a normal color but runny, then your ferret may have simple diarrhea. This may be caused by a sudden change in food, or by giving it the wrong foods such as milk or certain treats. If this seems a likely cause, and your ferret is well in other ways, give your ferret a very plain diet for a day or so, with no treats. This will often give its stomach a rest and fix things.

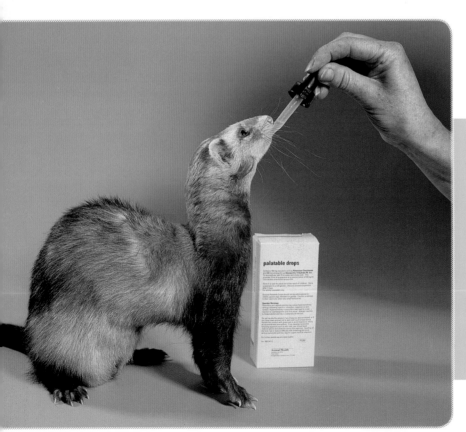

palatable drops

For some problems, your ferret may need to take some medicine. One of the easiest ways to give it medicine is to use a dropper. Medicine should always be kept in a place where your ferret cannot reach it.

If your ferret's feces are very unusual, such as greenish colored, jelly-like, very smelly, or if they have blood in them, your ferret may have an infection. You will need to see a vet quickly. Dark, thread-like feces sometimes mean the ferret has eaten something that has blocked its intestines. Again, you should get to your vet quickly.

Toothache

Ferrets often chip their teeth when they are playing. A chipped tooth will discolor and turn gray over time. This is not a problem unless it causes pain. A ferret with a toothache may paw at its mouth and be obviously in pain when it eats. It may also not eat its food, drool, and look uncomfortable. Your ferret may need to have a tooth extracted (taken out). Your vet will give your ferret a general anesthetic to put it to sleep for a short time while the painful tooth is being removed.

BAD BREATH

Bad breath is usually caused by bad teeth or infected gums. It is not common in younger ferrets that have been fed a correct diet, but older ferrets sometimes develop this problem.

Check your ferret's mouth at least once a week. Red, sore-looking gums mean an infection. Your vet will give your ferret medicine to cure the infection. If your ferret's teeth are dirty, the vet will clean them.

Dirty ears

A little yellowish-brown wax in your ferret's ears is normal. Dark-brown, gritty-looking wax may mean a ferret has **ear-mites**. These are tiny creatures that can cause pain and discomfort to your ferret. Ear-mites can be easily treated with ear drops from your vet. If left untreated, ear-mites may travel deep into your ferret's ear, causing it to lose its sense of balance. If your ferret has itchy ears, or holds its head tilted to one side, it needs urgent treatment. Weekly ear checks will catch any mite problem early and prevent serious problems.

Colds

You are very unlikely to catch anything from your ferret, but your pet might catch an illness from you. Ferrets often catch human colds and flu, and **kits** or older ferrets may even die. A sick ferret will have similar symptoms to you—a cough, sneezing, runny eyes and nose, and a temperature. It will need a visit to the vet and some gentle nursing.

If you have a cold, handle your ferret as little as possible or get someone else to care for your pet until you are better.

Wounds, bites, and stings

Ferrets can get themselves into trouble and get hurt. They may also be stung by a wasp or a bee if one gets into their cage. Usually all that is needed is to clean the area with a mild antiseptic. Make sure you remove any stinger or object still stuck in the wound. If you cannot remove it, you must take your pet to the vet to have it removed. You must watch any wounds, bites, or stings to make sure an **abscess** does not form. This is a swelling that contains pus, and it will need to be broken, drained, and cleaned by your vet.

If your ferret cuts itself, clean the wound with a mild antiseptic. A soothing, pet-safe ointment can help, too.

HAIR LOSS

Heavy hair loss is common when ferrets **molt**. They sometimes end up with bald tails!

✪ Hair loss usually only lasts for a few weeks and is nothing to worry about, as long as the ferret is otherwise fit and well.

✪ If your ferret becomes bald elsewhere, especially on the back and sides of its body, it might be something more serious and you should take it to a vet.

Parasites

Sometimes your ferret may have **internal parasites** such as **worms** living inside its intestines. Parasites can be caught by eating raw meat or dead animals. Even if you do not feed these to your ferret, it may still pick something up (such as a dead mouse) when it is out on a walk.

External parasites, such as fleas and **ticks**, live on the ferret's skin. Fleas can be picked up from other animals, and ticks from bushes and other vegetation. You can protect your ferret from parasites by regular **worming** and flea and tick treatments. Your vet or a ferret club will be happy to advise you on this.

This is a magnified photograph of a tick. Ticks cling onto your ferret's skin and suck its blood. Your vet can give you something to help get rid of them.

Heatstroke

Ferrets do not pant or sweat, so they get very hot very quickly. This can be dangerous. A ferret can collapse from **heatstroke** in temperatures of around 27°Celsius (80°Fahrenheit). Help your ferret in an outside cage stay cool by providing lots of shade at all times of the day, a water bowl to splash in, and a damp towel to rub itself on. If your ferret is affected by the heat, roll it up in some cool, damp cloths and take it to a vet.

Lumps

Ferrets can get lumps and bumps just about anywhere on their body, although the stomach and neck are common places. Vets may be able to treat these. They may be abscesses and can be drained and cleaned, or they may be fatty lumps that are **benign** (not dangerous). In some cases a lump may be **cancerous** and will need to be cut out, if possible.

DANGER SIGNS

You should tell an adult and contact a vet immediately:

- ✪ if there is blood in your ferret's feces, or you see blood coming from your ferret's mouth, ears, nose, or bottom.

- ✪ if your ferret won't eat its food or starts to vomit (throw up).

- ✪ if your ferret suddenly collapses.

- ✪ if you suspect that your pet has a broken bone (for example, after a fall, or if your ferret has been crushed).

- ✪ if your ferret seems to be in pain when it goes to the bathroom.

- ✪ if your ferret's stomach suddenly becomes much bigger.

- ✪ if your ferret has a high temperature and is obviously in pain.

- ✪ if your ferret has an open wound or an abscess.

If you find a lump on your ferret, it is best to let a vet check it out.

Saying Goodbye

Most ferrets only live for seven or eight years, so no matter how well you care for your pet, one day it will die. Sometimes a ferret will die peacefully and unexpectedly at home. This will come as a shock for you, but do not blame yourself. There is probably nothing that you could have done to keep it alive.

A peaceful end

As a caring owner, the hardest responsibility of all is to know when to let your pet be **put down** to save it from suffering. Your ferret may be in a lot of pain caused by a serious illness that cannot be cured. Your vet will give it a small injection. This does not hurt. Your ferret will become **unconscious** and its heart will stop beating.

When ferrets get old, they become less energetic and spend more time sleeping.

FEELING UPSET

No matter how it happens, you will feel upset when a pet dies, especially if your ferret has been a friend for many years. It is perfectly normal for people—adults as well as children—to cry when a pet dies, or when they think of a dead pet. Eventually the pain will pass, and you will be left with happy memories of your pet.

Sometimes it helps to have a special burial place for your pet.

Caring for your pet will have taught you a lot about ferrets. Maybe you will be able to give a home to another ferret that needs love and care.

Keeping a Record

It is fun to keep a record of your ferret, just like a family photo album! You can look back at it and remind yourself of what you did together as you and your ferret grew up.

Maybe you could start with a picture or the story of the first day your ferret came to live with you. How big was it? How did it change over the first year you had it? Did it look different in the summer and the winter?

Important dates

Keep a diary of important dates for your pet's health, such as its **vaccination** dates and **worming** dates. It is also worth recording how your ferret's weight changes so that you can tell if it has gained more weight (or lost more weight) than it did the previous year. When you take your ferret to the vet, take your scrapbook with you. It could be very useful.

Perhaps you could take notes on the shows you went to with your ferret—and the prizes it won!

SHARING THE FUN

Collect magazine articles on ferrets. Cut them out and keep them in your scrapbook.

OWNER RESPONSIBILITY

Some ferret owners decide they no longer want their animals. Instead of finding caring new homes or giving them to a ferret rescue group, they turn the animals loose. The released ferrets have almost no chance of survival. Because ferrets have been pets for hundreds of years, they do not have the ability to live without the care of humans.

Whenever we get a pet, we are responsible for its health, happiness, and safety. We must promise that we will keep that pet and care for it for all of its life. Sharing your scrapbook with others will help teach that lesson.

Glossary

abscess   soft lump full of infected liquid called pus, often caused by a bite or sting

benign   not dangerous

board   care for an animal while its owner is away

breed   mate and then give birth to young

cancerous   caused by cancer

canine distemper   serious disease, similar to the flu, that can kill dogs, ferrets, and some other animals

carnivorous   mainly meat-eating

castration   operation to stop male ferrets from breeding

de-scent   surgical procedure to remove a ferret's scent glands

domesticate   tame an animal so that it can live with humans

ear-mite   small, spider-like creature that burrows into some animals' ears

external parasite   small creature, such as a tick, that lives on the body or in the fur of another animal

extinct   completely wiped out, with no living animals or plants of that species (type) left

feces   solid waste matter passed out of the body (also called droppings or stools)

groom   clean an animal's coat. Animals often groom themselves.

harness   set of straps that fits around an animal's body so that you can lead it when you take it for walks

heatstroke   illness caused by being too hot

hob   male ferret

housebreak   train an animal to use a litter tray or special toilet area

hygienic   clean and free from germs

inquisitive   interested in a lot of things and wanting to find out more

insure   pay regular money to a company so that it will pay for the cost if you have an accident or a problem

internal parasite   small creature, such as a worm, that lives inside the body of another animal

jill   female ferret

kit   young ferret

mammal   animal with fur or hair on its body that feeds its babies with milk

molt   lose hair at particular times of the year, usually spring or summer

mustelid   member of the weasel family, such as a polecat or a ferret, that has special scent glands that produce a strong smell

neuter   perform an operation that stops ferrets from having babies

nocturnal   active at night

protein   important part of an animal's diet that helps it to grow and to stay healthy

put down   give a sick animal an injection to help it die peacefully and without pain

spaying   surgical procedure that stops female animals from having babies

tarpaulin   thick, waterproof cloth

tick   small creature that lives in the fur of another animal

unconscious   not awake or aware of anything, as if in a deep sleep

vaccinate   give an injection that protects against a disease

vitamin   important substance found in food that helps people and animals to stay healthy

vitamin supplement   medicine or pill that provides extra vitamins

warm-blooded   able to create body heat

worm   (noun) internal parasite that lives in the intestines of animals

worm   (verb) treat an animal in order to get rid of internal parasites, such as worms

Find Out More

Books

There are not many books on ferrets written for young readers, but you may find the following books helpful:

Bucsis, Gerry, and Barbara Somerville. *Training Your Pet Ferret.* Hauppauge, N.Y.: Barron's, 2010.

McKimmey, Vickie. *Ferrets.* Neptune City, N.J.: T. F. H., 2009.

Morton, E. Lynn, and Christine Mathis. *Ferrets: A Complete Pet Owner's Manual.* Hauppauge, N.Y.: Barron's, 2010.

Websites

www.ferret.org
The American Ferret Association website contains lots of information about ferrets and how to care for them. You can also learn about shows and events, as well as shelters and vets.

www.ferretcentral.org
This website is full of helpful advice on caring for your ferret. It also provides lists of local clubs and shelters.

Index

abscesses 39, 41

bad breath 37
bathing 20
bed and bedding 14, 20
black-footed ferret 7
breeding 10, 35
buying your ferret 5, 11

cage 9, 12–13, 14
cage cleaning 20, 23
choosing your ferret 10–11
colds and flu 38

death 42–43
de-scenting 10, 34
diarrhea 36

ear-mites 38
ears 22, 38
exercise 16, 29

feces 22, 23, 36, 37, 41
"ferret-proofing" your home 16
fleas and ticks 14, 22, 33, 40
food and water 9, 15, 18–19
friendship 24–25, 27

grooming 20

hair loss 39
hammocks 14, 15, 20, 30
handling your ferret 11, 24, 26
harness 8, 23, 32
health 22, 34–41
heatstroke 13, 40

hobs (male ferrets) 7, 10, 35
housebreaking 6
hunting 5, 6, 25

indoors, living 13
infections 37
insurance 5

jills (female ferrets) 7, 10, 35

kits (young ferrets) 7, 11, 26, 35, 38

life span 7, 8, 42
litter corner 15, 20, 22, 36
lumps and bumps 22, 41

medicine, taking 36
molting 20, 39
mustelid family 4

nail care 21, 22
neutered ferrets 9, 10, 34, 35
nips and bites 9, 26–27

older ferrets 37, 38, 42
outdoors, living 13, 17
owning more than one ferret 10, 28

parasites 40
pet carriers 23
pets, other 25
playtime 9, 15, 16, 17, 28–31

polecats 4
proteins 18

rescue centers 25, 29, 45

safety 31, 32
scent glands 4, 10, 34
scrapbook 44–45
shampoo 20–21
smell 4, 9

teeth and gums 22, 37
toilet habits 6, 8, 15
toothache 37
toys 14, 30, 31
treats 19, 21, 36
tubes and tunnels 14, 29, 30

vacation care 23
vaccinations 9, 23, 34, 44
vets 9, 34, 37, 38, 39, 40, 41, 42, 44
vitamins 18, 19, 21

walks 8, 32–33
weight 6, 19, 44
worming 40, 44
wounds, bites, and stings 39

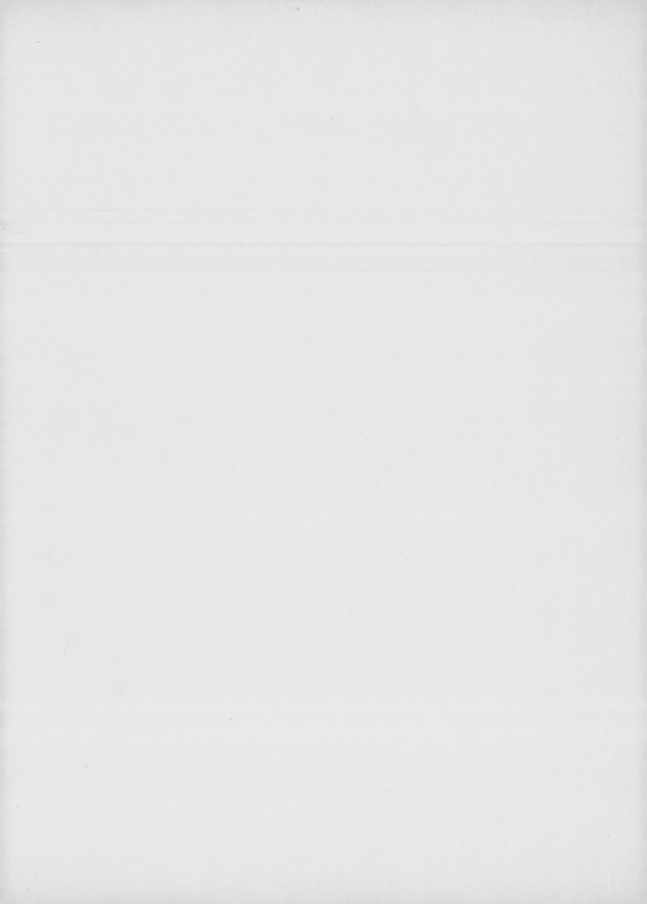